COLLECTED SHORT PLAYS

Books by Nathaniel Hutner

Heracleitus Under Water   1988

War: A Book Of Poems   2003

The Name We Never Lose   2019

The Complete Poems of Nathaniel Hutner   2021

☙

Plays by Nathaniel Hutner

Godot Arrives

Godot Imagine Godot

Godot at Night

Godot, Alive or Dead

The President Pardons Godot

☙

Short Plays by Nathaniel Hutner

Hot Potatoes

The Fix

Keewaydin Plays

Collected Short Plays

৪১

By Nathaniel Hutner

Burlington, Vermont

A collected edition of Nathaniel Hutner's plays, ***The Collected Plays of Nathaniel Hutner***, is available from Onion River Press, 191 Bank Street, Burlington, VT 05401

Copyright © 2021 by Nathaniel Hutner

All rights reserved. No part of this publication may be reproduced, distributed, or transmitted in any form or by any means, including photocopying, recording, or other electronic or mechanical methods, without the prior written permission of the publisher, except in the case of brief quotations embodied in critical reviews and certain other noncommercial uses permitted by copyright law.

Onion River Press
191 Bank Street
Burlington, VT 05401

ISBN: 978-1-949066-93-7

Library of Congress Control Number: 2021913979

Designed by Jenny Lyons, Middlebury VT

COLLECTED SHORT PLAYS

CONTENTS

HOT POTATOES 1

THE FIX 15

KEEWAYDIN PLAYS 29

Hot Potatoes

CAST OF CHARACTERS

TALLULAH: Tallulah Bankhead

FRANK: Her boyfriend

SCENE I

A kitchen in FRANK'S apartment, with all the accoutrements necessary for making potato pancakes: scrapers, knives, potatoes, onion, et cetera. As the scene begins we see TALLULAH stage right, dressed in evening clothes, apparently ready to go out for dinner. FRANK stands behind or alongside a kitchen counter happily working at his pancakes, paying little attention to TALLULAH.

> TALLULAH
> Darling, what's that you're doing?

> FRANK
> I'm peeling potatoes.

> TALLULAH
> For what? Are you on K.P.?

> FRANK
> K.P.?

> TALLULAH
> Yes. K.P. Kitchen Patrol. Weren't you ever in the army? I was.

> FRANK
> Coast Guard.

> TALLULAH
> They don't eat potatoes?

> FRANK
> They eat fish.

> TALLULAH
> I should have known. Why don't we go out to dinner?

FRANK
I want you to taste my potato pancakes. I'm using an old family recipe.

TALLULAH
Potato pancakes. Aren't they somewhat plebeian?

FRANK
They are delicious. You eat them with applesauce. Absolute Heaven.

TALLULAH
I'd rather go out. There is a very nice Chinese restaurant down the block. Their cold sesame noodles are out of sight.

FRANK
Not for me. Anyway I'm almost halfway through. I can't stop now. Would you like to help?

TALLULAH
I don't think so. My daddy never taught me how to cook.

FRANK
What about your mother?

TALLULAH
My mother was never in a kitchen in her life. She hated kitchens.

FRANK
Did she eat well?

TALLULAH
Eating killed her.

FRANK
Oh, really? How?

TALLULAH
She ate a bad oyster. Are there oysters in this potato recipe?

FRANK
Certainly not. Oysters and potatoes don't mix. And I'm not out to kill you. You are in for a rare culinary treat.

TALLULAH
I prefer Chinese.

FRANK
Now, now. If it doesn't turn out well, we can always go out.

TALLULAH
Well, dinner at home is romantic, isn't it?

FRANK
What are you doing? No tampering with the chef while he's working. Ouch. You're pinching me.

TALLULAH
I'm just trying to see if there is a real man behind that apron.

FRANK
Of course I'm a real man. Who says I'm not?

TALLULAH
Well, if you are, prove it. Give me a kiss.

FRANK
I can't give you a kiss. I have potato all over my hands. What are you doing? Watch out! You're going to ruin my recipe. I'll kick you out of the kitchen if you don't behave.

TALLULAH
Darling, I love you when you cook. I just want a little kiss. Maybe a bigger kiss. Yes. Right there. Oooh. Let's keep going.

FRANK
Not now. I'm still working on the potatoes. The onion comes next.

TALLULAH
Onion? You're putting onion into these things?

FRANK
It's delicious. You'll love it. When cooked, onion has a very pleasant and subtle flavor. Don't you think?

TALLULAH
Onion makes me cry.

FRANK
Oh, well, move off. Over there. Yes. That's good. You shouldn't smell it from there.

TALLULAH
But I don't want to be away from you. I want to be up close. Where I can see the color of your eyes, where I can taste your lips and smell your hay-scented hair. You are so attractive, I cannot control myself. Please put away the onion and let me come back. Please.

FRANK
Not yet. I'm almost through with it. There. Now we just mix them all together, add two egg yolks and one white. Mix, mix, mix. Et voilà. German potato pancake batter. At the ready.

TALLULAH
How do you cook them?

FRANK
The same way I cook you, my dear, I turn up the heat.

TALLULAH
Ohh. Another kiss. I shall die of frustration. Darling, let's skip dinner altogether. It is so boring. Sitting down separated by such a big table. I like your lap better.

FRANK
Nonsense. Maybe for dessert. Don't be disappointed. The night is not even begun. I shall finish off these pancakes, we shall eat our dinner, and then I shall relieve you of all the frustration you may feel. What do you think about that?

TALLULAH
Fix the potatoes.

FRANK
I am. I am.

TALLULAH
You are such a sneak. I have never seen anyone take so long to declare his intentions. That's what you're doing, isn't it?

FRANK
Well...

TALLULAH
Let me sit in your lap.

FRANK
I haven't finished.

TALLULAH
Oh, come off it.

FRANK
There. Now. A kiss. Ohh. that was a long one. Ohh. Deep throat.

TALLULAH
Ouch.

FRANK
Just a love bite.

TALLULAH
Well, don't take my ear off. Wait. Let me get my ear-rings off.

FRANK
I'm waiting.

TALLULAH
I have to get it off, if you're going to be biting me.

FRANK
I'll stop.

TALLULAH
But I don't want you to stop. It feels so delicious. Oh, that was a nice one. Is anything happening in the downstairs department?

FRANK
Yes.

TALLULAH
Oohh, look at that.

FRANK
My pancakes!

TALLULAH
What about them?

FRANK
They're burning.

TALLULAH
Burning?

FRANK
Yes. Quick. Get off. There. Oh. Well. I'll just have to make some more.

TALLULAH
Don't you have more batter?

FRANK
Yes.

TALLULAH
Well.

FRANK
I'll make some more. There. Now this time don't distract me.

TALLULAH
Distract you?

FRANK
Yes. I must concentrate on my cooking.

TALLULAH
Well, I'm cooking too, and I may boil over. Why in Hades name can't you forget about your frigging potatoes and have some fun with me? I don't make myself available to just anyone.

FRANK
Darling, I know. I wanted to please you with dinner.

TALLULAH
You did. But it's just begun.

FRANK
Really?

TALLULAH
Yes. Now let me back in your lap. There. Let's try one of those big kisses. Really big. Ohh. That is good. You learn faster than most men half your age. Shall we proceed?

FRANK
Proceed?

TALLULAH
You don't think we stop here, do you?

FRANK
No.

TALLULAH
Where's the bedroom?

FRANK
Through there. I'll turn the pancakes.

TALLULAH
The pancakes, the pancakes.

FRANK
I think they're ready. Darling? Are you coming?

TALLULAH
Yes.

FRANK
Dinner is ready.

TALLULAH
You're not kidding. The pancakes runneth over. Come on over here, honey. We can save the pancakes for Christmas. Now. Off with the shirt. Thank you. Ohh, what a lovely chest. I always have liked understated muscles. A hint of brawn.

FRANK
I'm glad you like me.

TALLULAH
I don't know about the rest of you, honey, but so far you've got an incredible bod.

FRANK
I guess we don't know each other very well.

TALLULAH
I think we can take care of that. Now. Your pants. There. Very, very good. I adore muscular thighs. I called my last lover thunder-thighs. He loved it. Oh, I suppose I shouldn't talk about my past right now. And you're wearing bikini briefs. Look at what's inside...

(LIGHTS DOWN)

-FINIS-

The Fix

Based on a story by James Thurber, as told to me
by Ed Gallagher

CAST OF CHARACTERS

THE PRESIDENT OF THE UNITED STATES: A not very imposing gentleman nearing fifty, somewhat resembling Thomas E. Dewey

LIEUTENANT BRIAN COOLE: A war veteran, possibly 45, earthy, a loutish rogue

ATTENDANTS

SCENE I

An elegant sitting room atop the Waldorf-Astoria. A small bar stands stage right bearing a profusion of bottles, none of them full. As the scene opens, we see COOLE, stage left, sitting on a red settee drinking. A voice is heard offstage right.

    PRESIDENT
Where is he?

    ATTENDANT
In the sitting room. Drinking.

    PRESIDENT
Yes. What's his name?

    ATTENDANT
Coole. Lieutenant Brian Coole.

    PRESIDENT
This the door?

    ATTENDANT
No sir, here.

    PRESIDENT
Thank you.
(ATTENDANT can be heard going off. PRESIDENT enters sitting room. COOLE waves)

    PRESIDENT
How do you do?

    COOLE
Who the hell are you?

    PRESIDENT
The President.

COOLE
Of what?

PRESIDENT
The President of the United States.

COOLE
This is fine gin. Comes from Calcutta. Ever been in Inja? Full of corpses. And flies. The flies eat the corpses. But they have good gin. It keeps your mind off the corpses. If you drink enough, it keeps the flies off you. Pickled. See? President of the United States?

(PRESIDENT is at a loss)

COOLE
I thought so. New York is a dandy town, full of layabouts and frauds. How do I know you're not a fraud?

PRESIDENT
But this is the Waldorf.

COOLE
Phooey. You find frauds high and low. You could easily be my putrefied brother-in-law from Peoria looking for a handout, only I don't have a brother-in-law from Peoria. Wanna drink?
(COOLE takes one himself)

PRESIDENT
Now, look, I am the President…

COOLE
You don't look like him. Anyway, if you're the President, who am I?

PRESDIENT
You're…

COOLE
Ooooh, you don't know who I am.

PRESIDENT
Your name begins with a C.

COOLE
With a little further prompting, you may escape hanging. I'm an Irishman, and my name is...

PRESIDENT
... Coole!

COOLE
Bravo! You get the Medal of Honor.

PRESIDENT
But...

COOLE
Yes, you're here to award it to me. Have a drink.

PRESIDENT
I think I will.

COOLE
Yes. I have been a brave soldier, and you are here to give me a medal.

PRESIDENT
(Taking a drink)
Thank you.

COOLE
To my medal.

PRESIDENT
Yes.

COOLE
Don't you come with a bodyguard?

PRESIDENT
In the outer hall.

COOLE
Then you really are the President?

PRESIDENT
Yes, I think so.

COOLE
Good. Always happy to make a new acquaintance. Do you smoke?

PRESIDENT
No.

COOLE
Do you mind?
(COOLE pulls out a large cigar)

PRESIDENT
No.

COOLE
You are kind.
(Lights up)
Well, what's up?
(The PRESIDENT looks blank)

COOLE
A President and no small talk? I thought that was your stock-in-trade. Would you like to hear a joke?
(Proceeding)
If a raven brings a black baby, and a stork brings a white baby, what brings no baby? Give up? A swallow. I'll bet you never heard that one in your life. I only just heard it yesterday from a lady friend.
(The PRESIDENT looks increasingly pained)

COOLE
(Continuing)
Great girl. Anyways, now it's your turn.

PRESIDENT
I don't tell jokes.

COOLE
C'mon, it doesn't have to be dirty, just funny. C'mon.

PRESIDENT
(Stiffly)
I never tell jokes.

COOLE
Suit yourself, Mr. President. A little humor at the top would be a good thing for the Country. A little laugh keeps the mind open and the soul free. Are you a Republican or a Democrat?

PRESIDENT
What difference does that make?

COOLE
You should know better than I.

PRESIDENT
God.

COOLE
He is neither a Republican nor a Democrat. Well, I suppose you are ecumenical in pol.itics, and a good thing, too. Broad minds are a scarce commodity. But I do think you could develop your sense of humor.

PRESIDENT
What are we giving you this Medal for?

COOLE
Oh, I shot a few jerries in the Second War, and then saved my men in Korea by shipping out God knows how many chinks on a hilltop. It was swell.

PRESIDENT
Are you retired?

COOLE
Yup.

PRESIDENT
Married?

COOLE
Nope.

PRESIDENT
Where do you live?

COOLE
Braintree.

PRESIDENT
Ahh.

COOLE
Beautiful town. I live with my sister. Great woman. Loves purple dressing gowns. Husband left her.

PRESIDENT
Too bad.

COOLE
Yes.

PRESIDENT
You seem to be happy here, there.

COOLE
Very.

PRESIDENT
Look. I'm the President and I think you should be civil.

COOLE
I'm as civil as you.

PRESIDENT
Oh, shut up and have another.

COOLE
Thank you. Ever been to Braintree?

PRESIDENT
Haven't had the pleasure.

COOLE
Delightful place. Full of factories. They make shoes. See?
(COOLE shows the PRESIDENT his shoes)

PRESIDENT
Very nice.

COOLE
Another drink?

PRESIDENT
Ohh...

COOLE
Here. Ever shot anybody?

PRESIDENT
I went hunting once.

COOLE
Yeah. Hit anything?

PRESIDENT
My foot.

COOLE
You're the President. How about people?

PRESIDENT
What?

COOLE
Ever hoot a human being?

PRESIDENT
Well...

COOLE
I can see you haven't. It would show if you had. Ever been in a war?

PRESIDENT
I make wars.

COOLE
A real politician. I'm a drinker. What's your name, Mr. President?

PRESIDENT
Charles.

COOLE
Shoot-em up Charlie. That's you. You send the likes of us out to die and hang medals on our corpses.

PRESIDENT
Would you prefer politics?

COOLE
Yes. Well. Another drink?

PRESIDENT
You're very kind, but no thank you. I must be going. When do we start the ceremony?

COOLE
Four o'clock, they say.

PRESIDENT
It's a quarter to.

COOLE
I'll see you downstairs.

PRESIDENT
Yes.
(PRESIDENT exits and meets two attendants in the hall)

PRESIDENT
Get rid of him, any way you can.
(ATTENDANTS enter sitting room and after a brief struggle, throw COOLE out the window)
(It is four o'clock in the Waldorf ballroom)

PRESIDENT
Ladies and Gentlemen, it saddens me to tell you that the recipient of today's honor cannot be here to receive it. I have only now been informed that Lieutenant Brian Coole has fallen to his death from his suite on the thirteenth floor of this hotel. Lieutenant Coole and I knew each other only for a short time, yet I can say that he was a true hero, both in modesty and accomplishment. He killed literally dozens of Germans, in the Second World War, and in one Korean engagement, fought off at least one hundred enemy soldiers with his bare knuckles. Yet he lived in recent years in the comparative quiet of Braintree, Massachusetts, noted for its charming colonial houses. We shall all miss our hero, and I hope that you will pray with me that his soul may rise on a straight flight heavenward. Thank you.

-FINIS-

The Keewaydin Plays

The Cow: Part 1 and Part 2
A Dream

The Cow: Part 1 and Part 2

CAST OF CHARACTERS

MERRILY

POPS

COW

PART 1

>MERRILY

You don't need a whole cow. We are not pigs.

>POPS

You cannot get milk from half a cow.

>MERRILY

Yes you can—the back half. Everybody does it. It is routine

>POPS

So you cut the poor beast in half? It will have only two legs to stand on while we milk.

>MERRILY

That's all that most people stand on.

>POPS

But the back half of a cow?

>MERRILY

We will train it.

>POPS

Good luck.

>MERRILY

I am an experienced trainer. I have been standing on two legs almost since I was born.

>POPS

What are the results?

>MERRILY

Can't you tell?
(She stands on one leg and tries to look like a crane resting—and she succeeds very well)

POPS
Hurrah! How long can you go like that?

MERRILY
Five minutes. I just need time enough to make my point.

POPS
Oh.

MERRILY
Now, about the cow...

POPS
(COW appears)
Oh!

MERRILY
What a dainty cow!

POPS
Reminds me of my aunt Sarah Jerusha.

MERRILY
Who?

POPS
A relative.

MERRILY
You're related to a cow?

POPS
Yes.

MERRILY
Family trees are so complicated. Mine includes two orangutans.

POPS
So I see.

MERRILY
And on my mother's side we have lots of Footes.

POPS
Feet.

MERRILY
No. F-O-O-T-E-S.

POPS
Oh.
(Lights up pipe)

MERRILY
You're polluting the environment.

POPS
Only the immediate environment.

MERRILY
Well, at Keewaydin we like to set a good example. The production of smoke is not attractive or healthy. For anybody.

POPS
Thanks for the lecture.

MERRILY
(Having second thoughts)
I guess a pipe is alright. It has a wonderful aroma.
(POPS smiles)
And I know you don't inhale, so I won't complain. Besides, it makes you look like Santa Claus.

POPS
Camouflage.

MERRILY
May I try?
(She takes the pipe and puffs once. She immediately starts coughing violently)

POPS
You need experience. I am a good trainer. I have been smoking a pipe almost since I was born.

MERRILY
I shall stick to bubble gum.

POPS
It gives you sweet breath.

MERRILY
And rotten teeth.

POPS
Heavens! What you get from one hand, the other hand taketh away.

MERRILY
Lemonade is nice.

POPS
Not bad.

MERRILY
Fresh spring water.

POPS
Ahh!

MERRILY
A rainbow trout pan-broiled at dusk, with embers glowing below the smoke.

POPS
Splendid.

MERRILY
Sticky buns.

POPS
My favorite anytime.

MERRILY
We have much to be thankful for.

POPS
Besides ourselves.

MERRILY
Yes. Look at all those people.
(Gestures toward the audience)

POPS
I know. They are our friends.

MERRILY
We ARE lucky.

-FINIS-

PART 2

MERRILY
This cow has laid an egg!

POPS
Impossible.

MERRILY
Why not? Anyone can lay an egg—with practice.

POPS
Some do it without practice.

MERRILY
What do you do once the egg is laid?

POPS
Have it for breakfast.

MERRILY
This one's very big.

POPS
Have it for dinner. Invite guests.

MERRILY
It's been sitting around for weeks.

POPS
It smells gaseous.

MERRILY
Aha!

POPS
What?

MERRILY
If it is gaseous, we can blow it up on July 4th, which is very soon. It will make a wonderful spectacle.

POPS
Brilliant. Does your cow have any other hidden talents?

MERRILY
Oh, I don't know. Sometimes it loses a spot or two: they fall off.

POPS
Must be a Holstein. We can call it Spot.

MERRILY
It's a bit big to be called Spot. Spot is for dogs.

POPS
Do you see a dog around here?
(They look for a dog)

MERRILY
Well, Pops, what would you name our cow?

POPS
Spot won't do?

MERRILY
Nope.

POPS
Fido. That's Latin for Faith.

MERRILY
I give up.

POPS
OK, how about Gertrude?

MERRILY
Excellent. If I have any children, you get to be godfather.

POPS
Do we baptize the cow?

MERRILY
Here's some milk.
(The COW gets wet)

POPS
I hereby baptise you: Gertrude.
(The COW moos happily)

MERRILY
I knew we chose the right name.

POPS
Does it have relatives? I have some milk left.

MERRILY
Drink it for breakfast.

POPS
Milk and eggs.

MERRILY
One egg, and not fresh.

POPS
Look at the balloon!

MERRILY
It's my birthday.

POPS
Congratulations. You have now lasted as long as the Peloponnesian War.

MERRILY
I am not at all sure that that is a good thing.

POPS
Age is what you make of it.

MERRILY
So is Keewaydin.

POPS
Your cow is quite handsome.

MERRILY
She is young and full of milk.

POPS
Can we expect any more eggs?

MERRILY
Certainly not. Eggs are not predictable, especially when they are laid by someone you know.

POPS
They take you by surprise.

MERRILY
With most people, yes.

POPS
Yet there are some—

MERRILY
There are some you can smell a mile away.

POPS
I shall be prepared.

MERRILY
Good idea.

POPS
Life here is almost ideal.

MERRILY
The cow is perfection.

POPS
You too.

(Hugs her)
MERRILY
(Turning to audience)
What about our friends?
POPS
(To audience)
You too.

-FINIS-

A Dream

CAST OF CHARACTERS

ALFRED

BALDY

TOURIST GUIDE

ALFRED
Piracy?

BALDY
Pirates. I see them coming.
(Continuing)
In Tahiti?

ALFRED
We're in Tahiti?

BALDY
But that's the Battersea Power Station. We must be in London.

ALFRED
The Eiffel Tower!

BALDY
The Parthenon!

ALFRED
We must be dreaming!

BALDY
Or moving very fast.

ALFRED
Satellites move fast.

BALDY
Yes, I believe they can circle the earth quite quickly.

ALFRED
But we're not high up.

BALDY
Then it's all a dream.

ALFRED
I hope it doesn't end yet.

BALDY
Why?

ALFRED
Well, I've always wanted to see Beijing. The Chinese are a remarkable people—and their culture is the oldest living culture on earth.

BALDY
They are very fortunate. Think what history has taught them.

ALFRED
And poetry.
(BALDY looks doubtful)

BALDY
Do you know Chinese?

ALFRED
I know how to say hello.

BALDY
That's a start.

ALFRED
In Russian I can say Ya Vas Lublju.

BALDY
What does that mean?

ALFRED
I love you.

BALDY
Oooh — that will get you very far. Maybe you can use it in

China. I am sure they would understand.

ALFRED
The Chinese are wise. They certainly deserve as much as anyone else.

BALDY
Well, let's get this dream moved over there.
(They do)

ALFRED
The forbidden city?

BALDY
Beautiful.

ALFRED
Fascinating. I wonder if they have tours?

BALDY
In a dream, anything is possible.
(A tour guide appears)

MISS HONEYPOT
I am Miss Honeypot. And I am told you want a guide.

ALFRED
It would be helpful.

MISS HONEYPOT
Since you are having a dream, you may see whatever you wish.

ALFRED
Let me think. The Fort. Where did the Emperor put the Fort?

MISS HONEYPOT
Fort?

ALFRED
The loo, the WC.

MISS HONEYPOT
That is a very serious question. After all, the son of the Sun had to preserve his image.

BALDY
Like the Wizard of Oz.

ALFRED
Of course.

MISS HONEYPOT
Ah, here we are.

ALFRED
A bit small.

MISS HONEYPOT
So as to be inconspicuous.

BALDY
And easy to clean.

MISS HONEYPOT
Very important.

ALFRED
And the kitchens?

MISS HONEYPOT
Follow me.

ALFRED
Fabulous. I infer that the Emperor did not dine out. These arrangements are magnificent.

BALDY
They enjoyed their food.

MISS HONEYPOT
Yes. One of my ancestors was a beekeeper by appointment to the Imperial Court.

ALFRED
That explains your name?

MISS HONEYPOT
Yes.

ALFRED
What did they eat?

MISS HONEYPOT
Almost anything that could be cooked and would taste good without upsetting the digestion.

BALDY
They must have had a varied menu.

MISS HONEYPOT
Indeed.

ALFRED
I hear there was a court poet.

MISS HONEYPOT
Oh, yes. He was very popular, as he told the truth without anyone objecting.

BALDY
Impossible.

MISS HONEYPOT
Well, not everyone understood what he was saying.

BALDY
Not even the critics?

MISS HONEYPOT
They were somewhat obtuse — and they didn't like verse. It makes you think.

BALDY
Well some of us are on permanent vacation when it comes to thinking.

MISS HONEYPOT
Yes. Any other requests?

BALDY
The Fort and the Kitchen. We've seen the important stuff.

ALFRED
I would like to send a photo of the Throne Room back to camp.

BALDY
We don't have a throne room at camp.

ALFRED
We don't need one.

BALDY
Certainly not. Nature herself looks after us, and we take care of the rest without much interference from above.

MISS HONEYPOT
Sounds attractive.

ALFRED
Oh, it is a type of arrangement that is becoming increasingly fashionable, indeed popular all over the world.

MISS HONEY POT
Sensible.

ALFRED
Well it is only common sense, but some very famous people never had much common sense.

BALDY
No, but they had plenty of brains.

ALFRED
Yes, we try not to imitate them in every way.

MISS HONEYPOT
Well, that is good.

ALFRED
And where is the way out?

MISS HONEYPOT
Since this is a dream, you should close your eyes and tap your heels three times, and when you open your eyes, you will be at Keewaydin.

(They follow the instructions and wake up at camp)

-*FINIS*-

www.ingramcontent.com/pod-product-compliance
Lightning Source LLC
Chambersburg PA
CBHW030201100526
44592CB00009B/394